GRAPHIC HISTORY

THE BOSTON MASSACRE

by Michael Burgan

illustrated by Bob Wiacek,
Keith Williams, and
Charles Barnett III

Consultant:
Susan Goganian, Site Director
The Bostonian Society
Boston, Massachusetts

Capstone
press

Mankato, Minnesota

Graphic Library is published by Capstone Press,
1710 Roe Crest Drive, North Mankato, Minnesota 56003.
www.capstonepub.com

Library of Congress Cataloging-in-Publication Data
Burgan, Michael.
    The Boston Massacre / by Michael Burgan; illustrated by Bob Wiacek, Keith Williams,
and Charles Barnett III.
        p. cm.—(Graphic library. Graphic history)
    Includes bibliographical references and index.
    ISBN: 978-0-7368-4368-3 (hardcover)
    ISBN: 978-0-7368-6202-8 (softcover pbk.)
    1. Boston Massacre, 1770—Juvenile literature. I. Title. II. Series.
E215.4.B869 2006
973.3'113—dc22   2005006462

Summary: In graphic novel format, tells the story of the Boston Massacre.

Art and Editorial Direction
Jason Knudson and Blake A. Hoena

Designers
Jason Knudson and Ted Williams

Colorist
Brent Schoonover

Editor
Erika L. Shores

Editor's note: Direct quotations from primary sources are indicated by a yellow background.

Direct quotations appear on the following pages:
Pages 8, 13, 14, 19, 20, 26, from *The Boston Massacre* by Hiller B. Zobel (New York:
  W. W. Norton, 1970).
Page 10, from *Samuel Adams: The Fateful Years, 1764–1776* by Stewart Beach (New York:
  Dodd, Mead, and Company, 1965).
Page 25 (top), from *John Adams and the American Revolution* by Catherine Drinker Bowen
  (Boston: Little, Brown, and Company, 1950).
Page 25 (bottom), from John Adams' speech at the Boston Massacre trial (The Boston Massacre
  Historical Society, www.bostonmassacre.net/trial/acct-adams3.htm).

Printed and bound in the United States of America.
002273

TABLE OF CONTENTS

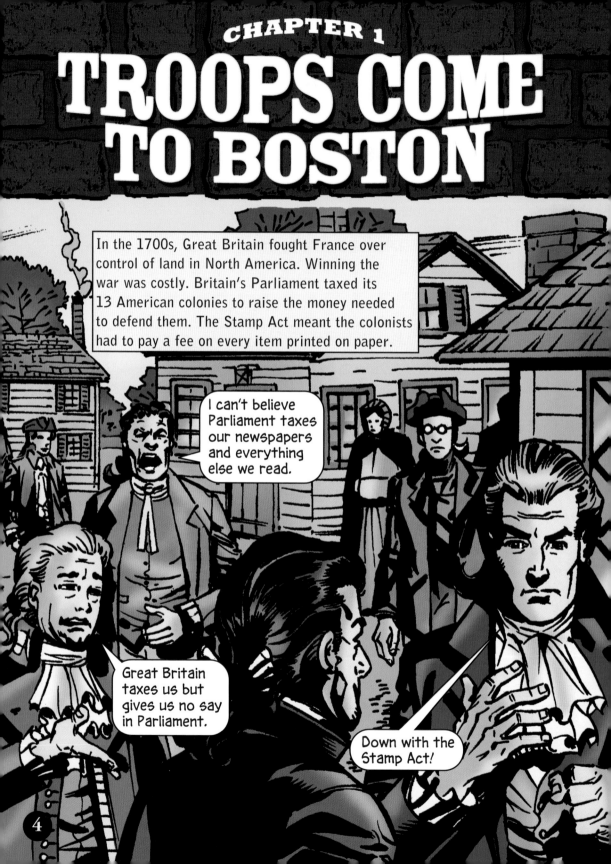

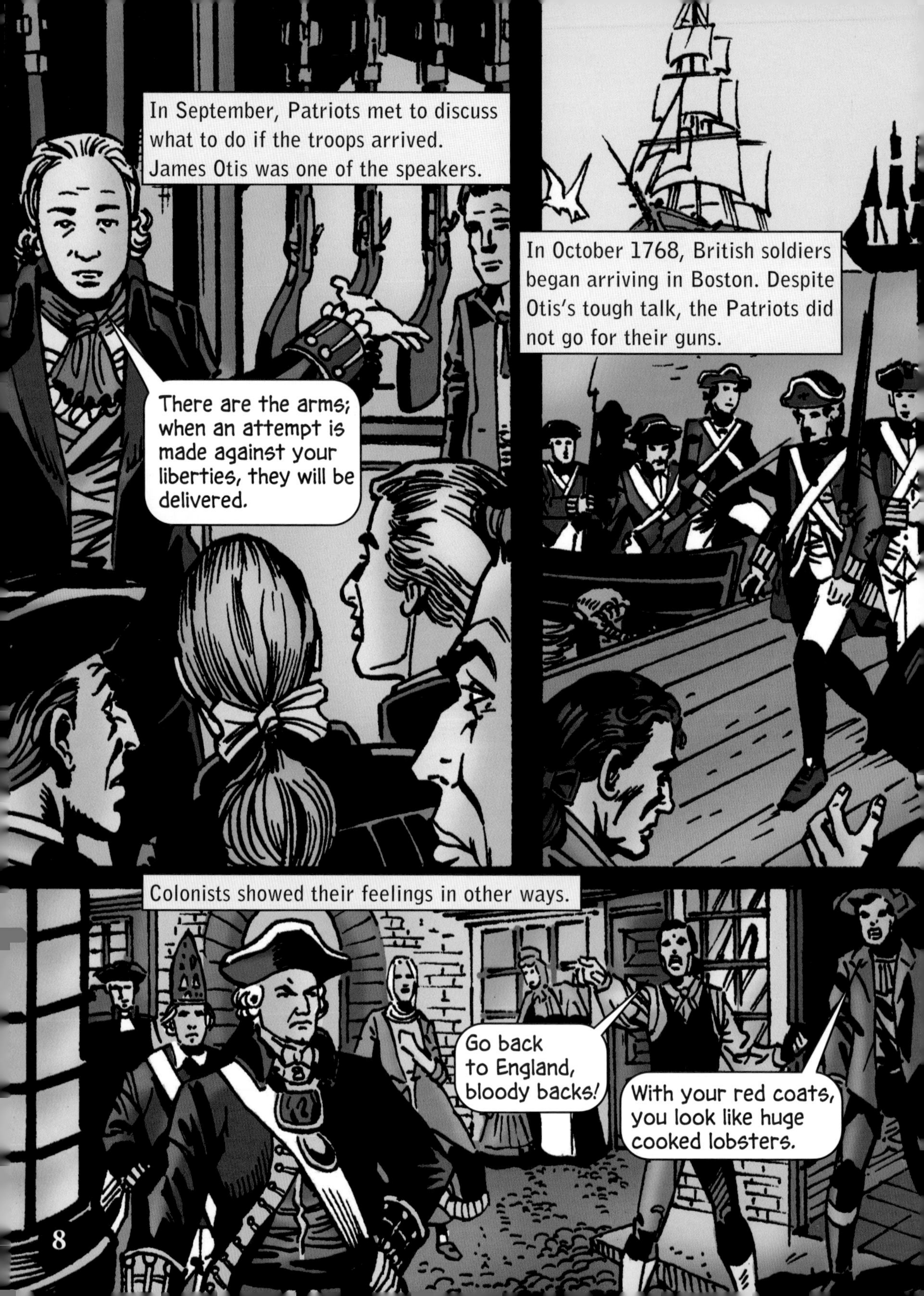
In September, Patriots met to discuss what to do if the troops arrived. James Otis was one of the speakers.
There are the arms; when an attempt is made against your liberties, they will be delivered.
In October 1768, British soldiers began arriving in Boston. Despite Otis's tough talk, the Patriots did not go for their guns.
Colonists showed their feelings in other ways.
Go back to England, bloody backs!
With your red coats, you look like huge cooked lobsters.

9

CHAPTER 2

SHOTS IN THE STREET

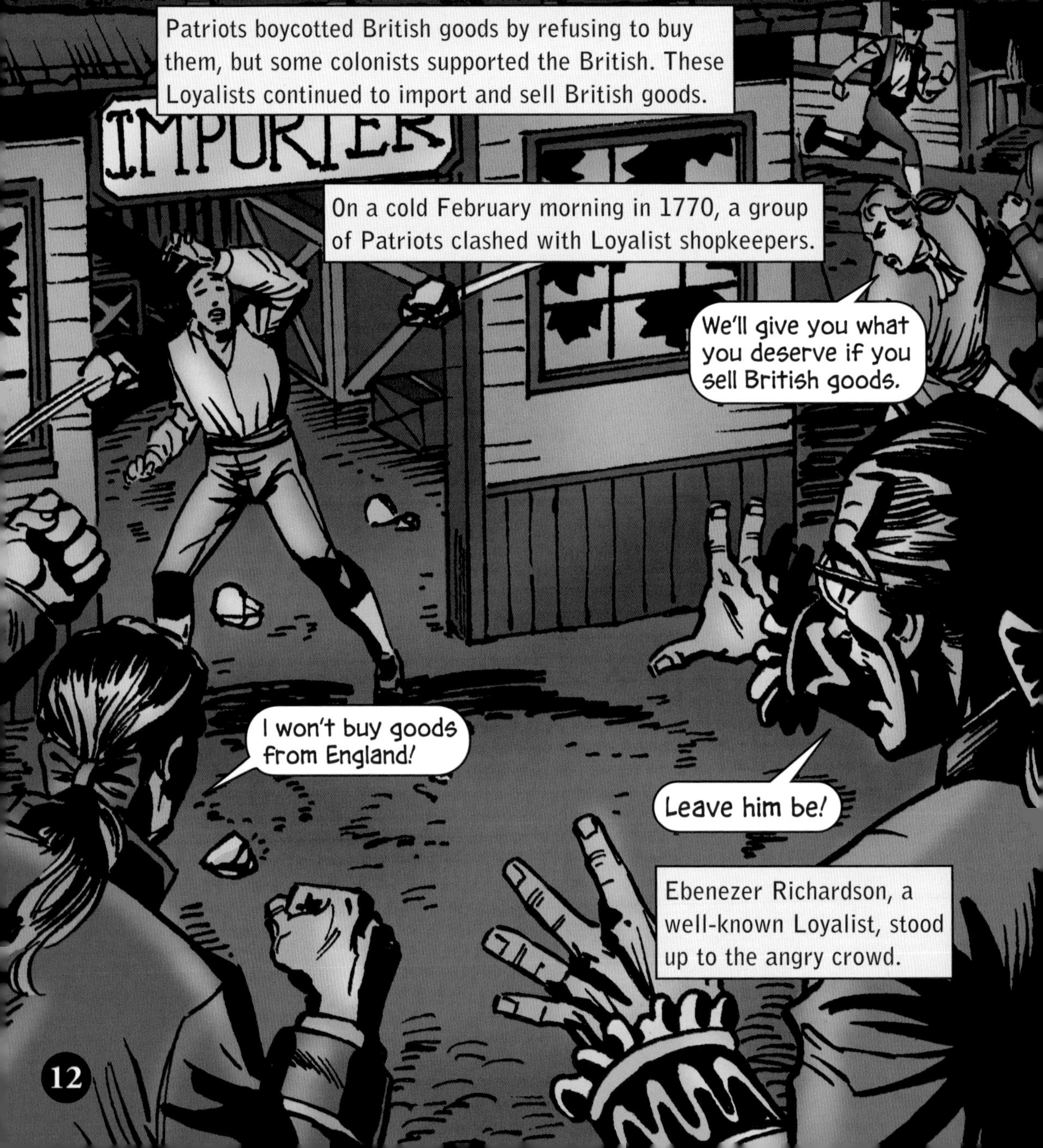
Patriots boycotted British goods by refusing to buy them, but some colonists supported the British. These Loyalists continued to import and sell British goods.
IMPORTER
On a cold February morning in 1770, a group of Patriots clashed with Loyalist shopkeepers.
We'll give you what you deserve if you sell British goods.
I won't buy goods from England!
Leave him be!
Ebenezer Richardson, a well-known Loyalist, stood up to the angry crowd.

13

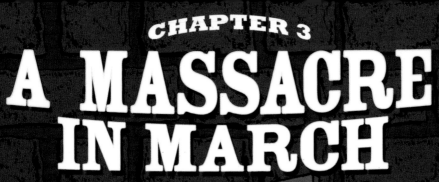

CHAPTER 3

A MASSACRE IN MARCH

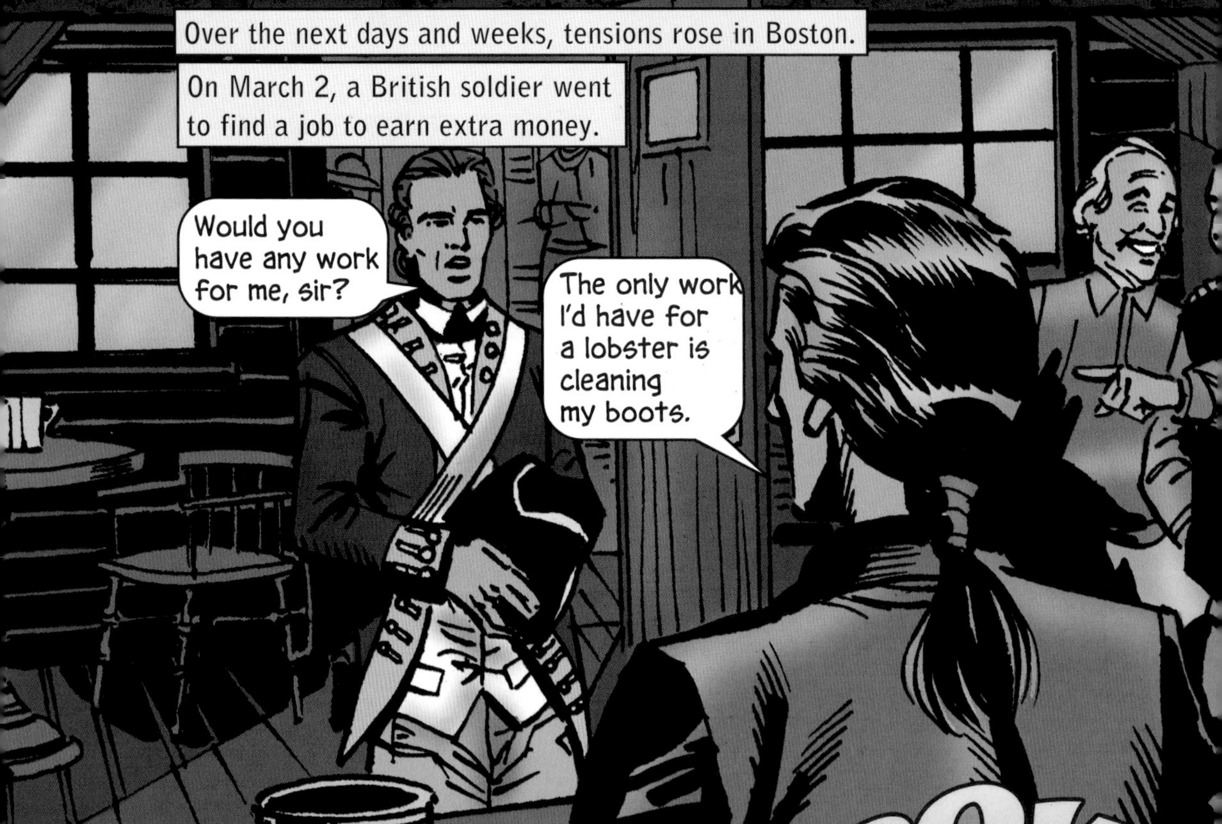
Over the next days and weeks, tensions rose in Boston.
On March 2, a British soldier went to find a job to earn extra money.
Would you have any work for me, sir?
The only work I'd have for a lobster is cleaning my boots.

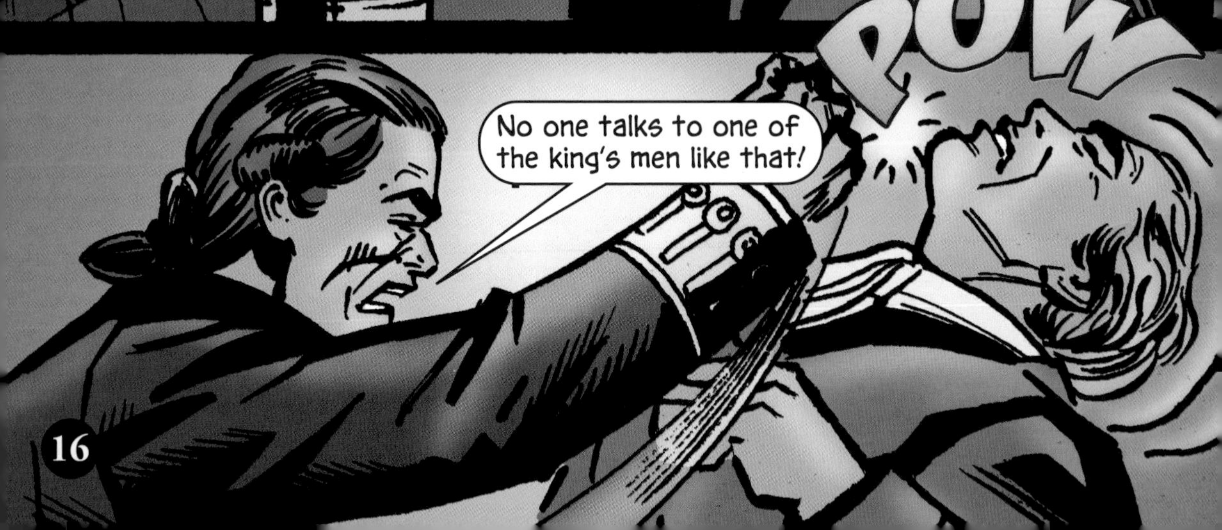
POW
No one talks to one of the king's men like that!

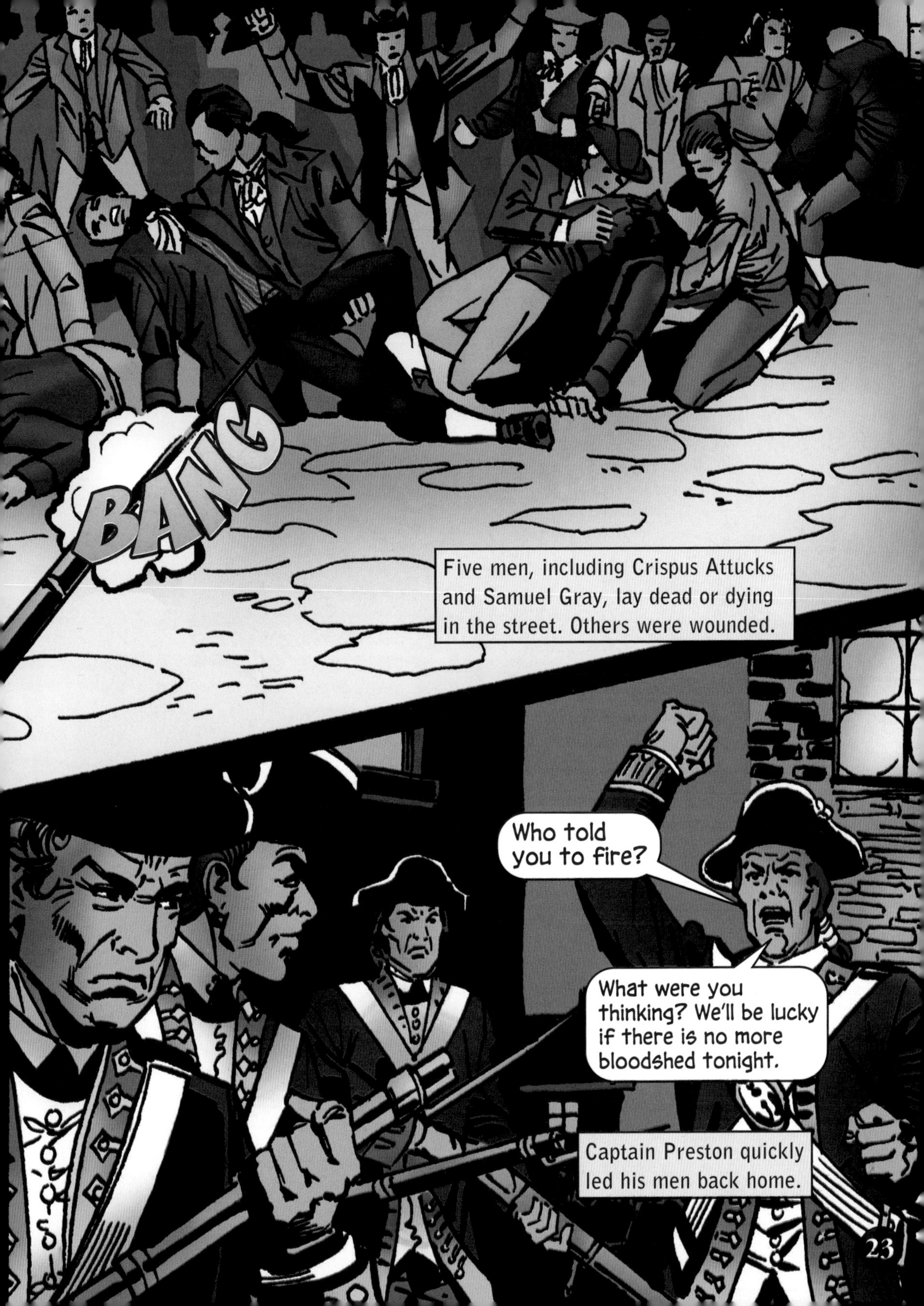
BANG
Five men, including Crispus Attucks and Samuel Gray, lay dead or dying in the street. Others were wounded.
Who told you to fire?
What were you thinking? We'll be lucky if there is no more bloodshed tonight.
Captain Preston quickly led his men back home.

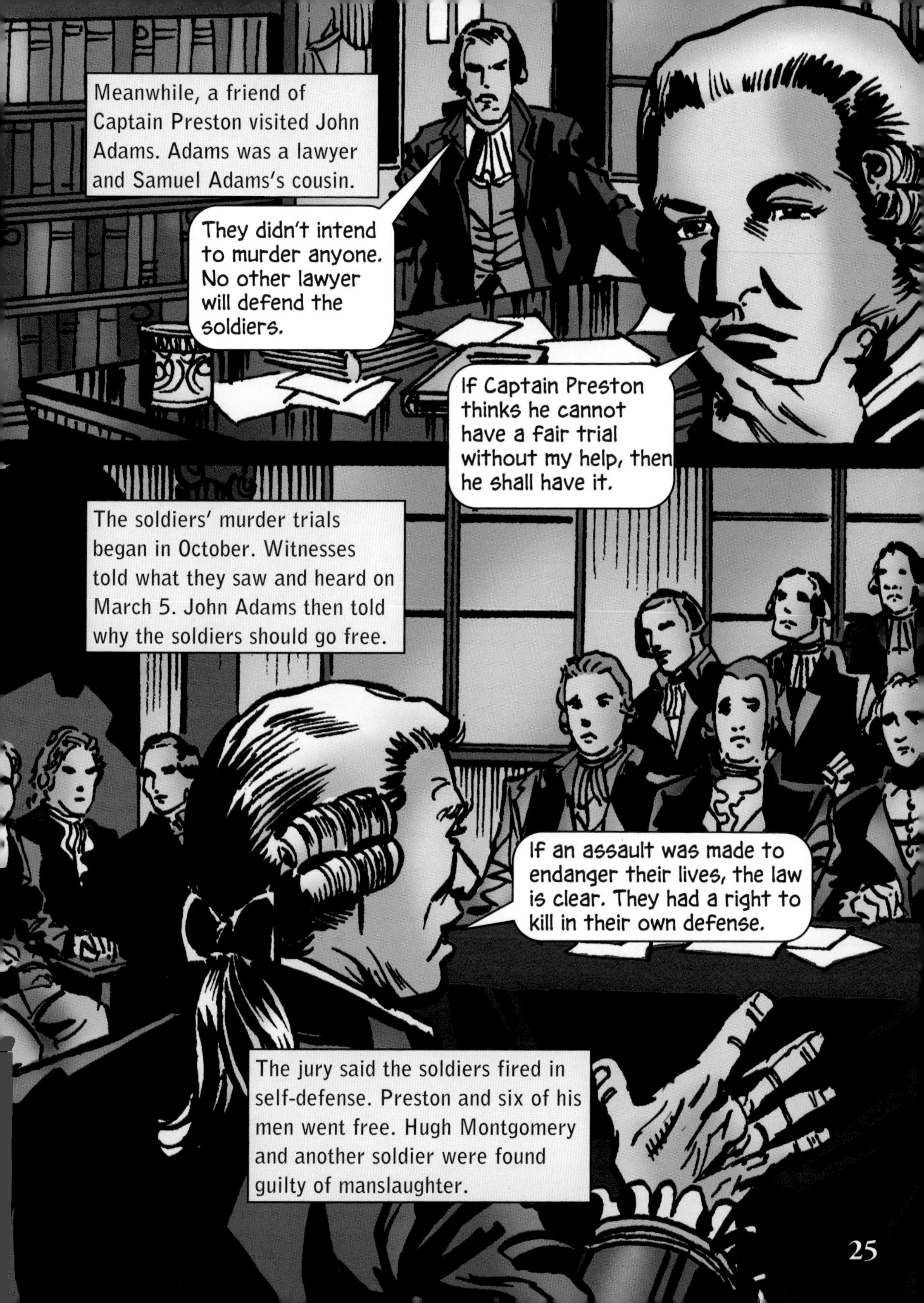
Meanwhile, a friend of Captain Preston visited John Adams. Adams was a lawyer and Samuel Adams's cousin.
They didn't intend to murder anyone. No other lawyer will defend the soldiers.
If Captain Preston thinks he cannot have a fair trial without my help, then he shall have it.
The soldiers' murder trials began in October. Witnesses told what they saw and heard on March 5. John Adams then told why the soldiers should go free.
If an assault was made to endanger their lives, the law is clear. They had a right to kill in their own defense.
The jury said the soldiers fired in self-defense. Preston and six of his men went free. Hugh Montgomery and another soldier were found guilty of manslaughter.

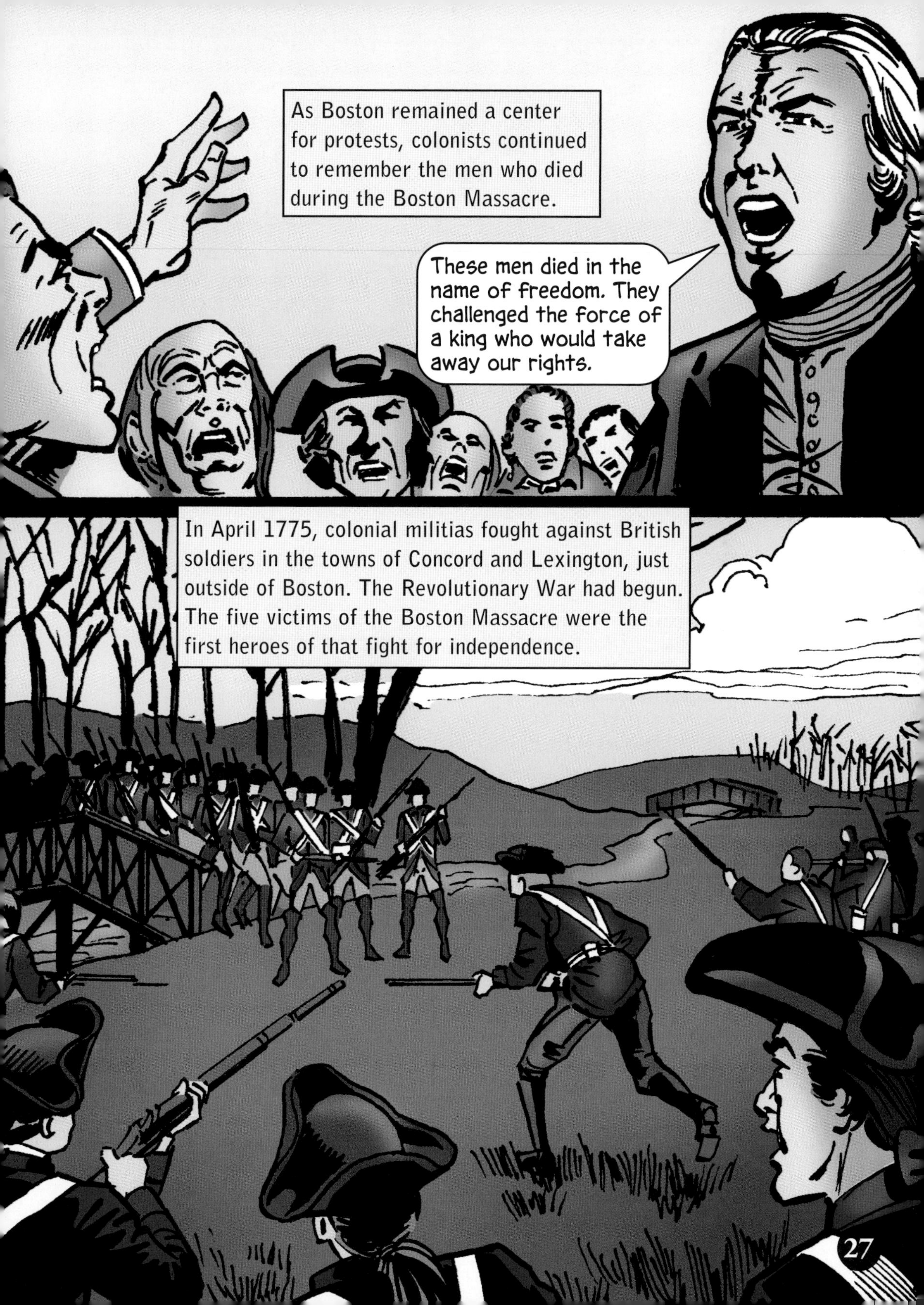
As Boston remained a center for protests, colonists continued to remember the men who died during the Boston Massacre.
These men died in the name of freedom. They challenged the force of a king who would take away our rights.
In April 1775, colonial militias fought against British soldiers in the towns of Concord and Lexington, just outside of Boston. The Revolutionary War had begun. The five victims of the Boston Massacre were the first heroes of that fight for independence.

MORE ABOUT THE BOSTON MASSACRE

- Crispus Attucks was the first man to die in the Boston Massacre. He was part Native American and part African American. A statue honoring Attucks stands in Boston Common, the largest park in Boston.

- The other victims of the Boston Massacre were Samuel Gray, Samuel Maverick, Patrick Carr, and James Caldwell. Maverick died the day after the massacre, and Carr died several days later.

- British soldiers Hugh Montgomery and Matthew Kilroy were found guilty of manslaughter for the deaths of Crispus Attucks and Samuel Gray. They could have been executed for their crime. Under British law, however, they were allowed to ask for special treatment. Instead of being killed, each man had a mark burned onto his right thumb with a hot iron.

After the Boston Massacre, Samuel and John Adams continued to play important roles in America's struggle for independence. Both wrote important articles explaining how British policies hurt the colonies. Samuel was one of the first Patriot leaders to call for independence. John later became the second president of the United States.

In colonial times, British law did not allow gatherings of more than 12 people in the streets. By reading aloud a law called the Riot Act, a British official could break up the crowd. If people didn't leave after the Riot Act was read, soldiers could fire into the crowd. Colonists on the streets of Boston thought they were safe the night of March 5, 1770. No one had read the Riot Act when the troops arrived.

A marker in Boston's Granary Burying Ground shows where the five victims of the Boston Massacre are buried. Eleven-year-old Christopher Seider is also buried there. His last name is incorrectly spelled "Snider" on the tombstone. Samuel Adams is also buried near these graves.

GLOSSARY

bayonet (BAY-uh-net)—a long metal blade attached to the end of a rifle

boycott (BOI-kot)—to refuse to buy something as a way of making a protest

import (IM-port)—to bring goods into a place or country from elsewhere

Loyalist (LOI-uh-list)—a colonist who was loyal to Great Britain before and during the Revolutionary War

manslaughter (MAN-slaw-tur)—the crime of killing someone without intending to do so

massacre (MASS-uh-kur)—the killing of a large number of people, often in battle

Parliament (PAR-luh-muhnt)—the governing body that makes the laws in Britain

Patriot (PAY-tree-uht)—a person who sided with the colonies before and during the Revolutionary War

smuggle (SMUHG-uhl)—to bring something in or out of a country illegally

INTERNET SITES

FactHound offers a safe, fun way to find Internet sites related to this book. All of the sites on FactHound have been researched by our staff.

Here's how:

1. Visit *www.facthound.com*
2. Type in this special code **073684368X** for age-appropriate sites. Or enter a search word related to this book for a more general search.
3. Click on the **Fetch It** button.

FactHound will fetch the best sites for you!

READ MORE

Draper, Allison Stark. *The Boston Massacre: Five Colonists Killed by British Soldiers.* Headlines from History. New York: PowerKids Press, 2001.

Mattern, Joanne. *The Cost of Freedom: Crispus Attucks and the Boston Massacre.* Great Moments in American History. New York: Rosen, 2003.

Ready, Dee. *The Boston Massacre.* Let Freedom Ring. Mankato, Minn.: Bridgestone Books, 2002.

Santella, Andrew. *The Boston Massacre.* Cornerstones of Freedom. New York: Children's Press, 2004.

BIBLIOGRAPHY

The Boston Historical Society and Museum
http://rfi.bostonhistory.org/

Boston Massacre Historical Society
http://www.bostonmassacre.net/

The Boston Massacre Trial of 1770
http://www.law.umkc.edu/faculty/projects/ftrials/bostonmassacre/bostonmassacre.html

Fleming, Thomas. *Liberty!: The American Revolution.* New York: Viking, 1997.

Langguth, A. J. *Patriots: The Men Who Started the American Revolution.* New York: Simon & Schuster, 1988.

Zobel, Hiller B. *The Boston Massacre.* New York: W. W. Norton, 1970.

INDEX